IMAGES
of America

THE
OLD ORCHARD

For centuries now, the beach at Old Orchard has beckoned people to its sandy shore. The Hotel Fiske, on the left, was one of the most majestic buildings on the Maine coast in the late 1800s. This photograph was taken between 1898 and 1907. How do I know? The pier, from which this shot was taken, opened on July 2, 1898, and the Hotel Fiske burned to the ground on August 15, 1907. All types of concessions and entertainment were available directly on the beach: one could have a fortune told by Queen Lillo (a palmist), snack on fresh roasted peanuts, or enjoy a hot bath in one of the many bath houses along the shoreline. (Ralph and Lois Duquette)

IMAGES
of America

THE
OLD ORCHARD

Jeffrey A. Scully

ARCADIA
PUBLISHING

Published by Arcadia Publishing
Charleston, South Carolina

Library of Congress Catalog Card Number: Applied for

For all general information contact Arcadia Publishing at:
Telephone 843-853-2070
Fax 843-853-0044
E-mail sales@arcadiapublishing.com
For customer service and orders:
Toll-Free 1-888-313-2665

Visit us on the Internet at www.arcadiapublishing.com

To Sharon Scully
My aunt and godmother; the person most responsible for expanding my
horizons and introducing me to Old Orchard and the Pine Tree State

(Jim Pate)

Contents

(Ralph and Lois Duquette)

Acknowledgments

As a book such as this is composed of a variety of photographs, so too, it is composed through the assistance of numerous people who have contributed their time, energy, and resources to see it through from start to finish. While there have been literally hundreds of conversations, phone calls, and personal contacts in compiling this volume, there have also been uncountable resources drawn upon for information to which credit cannot be directly given. Over the course of the past fifteen years that I have lived in this area, I have picked up tidbits here and there, and a general feeling for the history of Old Orchard. To anyone with whom I have chatted about the history of Old Orchard that is not listed here, I apologize and hope you will consider yourself to be remembered in the tomb of the unknown source.

But for those whom I name here, a mountain of gratitude is expressed. First and foremost, I wish to thank Mr. Dan Blaney, the closest thing to an official town historian I have ever met anywhere. When he writes his own history of the town of Old Orchard, I hope you will purchase a copy; it will be well worth the price. I would also like to thank the late Mr. Robert Murphy, former president of the Old Orchard Beach Historical Society, who passed away in the winter of 1995 (just prior to the completion of this book). Others I wish to thank, in no particular order of importance, include Ben and June Emery, Charles P. Swan, Jeanne Eddy, Shirley and Richard Doe, Richard Skillin, the Old Orchard Beach Historical Society, Ralph and Lois Duquette, Debbie Madden, Mr. and Mrs. J. Cobb, Mrs. Jackie Gelinas, Ms. Elaine Peverly, Jon Crook, Jim Pate, Earl Towle of the American Legion Post #57, Mrs. Teofila Macdonald, Nanci Boutet, Ruth Goodale Boutet, Alice Trull, Jack Trull, Mrs. Eileen McNally (librarian at the Libby Memorial Library in Old Orchard Beach), Steve Fregeau, Leo Boyle and the Maine Aviation Historic Society, Wil Browne, and the countless writers from various journals, pamphlets, magazines, newspapers, and town reports whose names have been lost over the years but who preserved the history of Old Orchard for generations to come, for which I and many others will be forever grateful.

(Ralph and Lois Duquette)

Foreword

History will note my first journey to Old Orchard Beach was on May 17, 1980, some 377 years after the British explorer Martin Pring first walked the sandy shore (I will admit that until that date, I had never heard of Old Orchard, or Martin Pring for that matter). Less than twenty-four hours earlier I had arrived in Maine at the Portland Jetport—it was my first trip to the Pine Tree State—with the intention of spending the entire summer living in Portland with my aunt, Sharon. I was so taken by the beauty of the beach that I nearly missed the other exciting event of the day: it wasn't until almost 3 p.m. that I remembered it was my twenty-second birthday.

I recall eating pizza and french fries; it was an odd combination of foods to me then, but one of the local customs I've grown to love. As I stood on the beach, my lily-white toes sinking into the sun-baked sand, I was a mid-western boy facing my first exposure to the multi-national fashion show, the bathing suits and bronzed bodies for which Old Orchard has become famous. I must admit that on that day, the fabled history of the town was the farthest thing from my mind. But some fifteen years later, I am infinitely more fascinated by this town's storied past than I ever could have imagined.

Of course, we all know a little local history about such things as the grand hotels, the pier, and the planes and cars that used the beach for recreation and entertainment. We have heard about the famous and near famous folks who have summered here, and we are all a little familiar with stories of fires, and the controversy surrounding condominiums and the Ballpark. Bits of folklore and gossip are casually tossed out to tourists and people "from away" like pieces of bread to flocking seagulls, but like Anytown, USA, the nitty-gritty, down and dirty history, the sordid details and juicy nuggets of a town's past take time to accumulate.

Old Orchard has certainly had its share of colorful history, and there is some of that here. Beyond this, however, I hope to provide some insight into the people responsible for the direction Old Orchard Beach has taken: a glimpse of the faces and places, some familiar and some long gone, that have been important to the area's history. Let your imagination pull you into the photographs; hear the sounds, smell the smells, taste the variety of flavors that make up the history of Old Orchard. Remember the first time you were in Old Orchard; perhaps you remember the heyday of the pier, riding on the Dummy Railroad, Lucky Lindy, and Benny Goodman. Or perhaps this is your first time here. Either way, I hope this book serves its purpose: to educate new visitors, and to entertain old, as the past is brought to the present.

Jeffrey A. Scully
February 23, 1995

Introduction

Of all the coastal destinations in Maine, there is none quite like Old Orchard. The crescent-shaped stretch of sandy beach that reaches from Goosefare Brook to Pine Point at the top of York County has always drawn people to it, from before the time British explorer Martin Pring first walked the beach in 1603 through to the present day. It has a long and storied history almost without equal on the Northeastern seaboard.

For those who are looking to this book as a definitive history of the town, I'm afraid you may be disappointed. It is not intended to be definitive: my hope is that it will provide a glimpse of what made Old Orchard famous around the world as a vacation destination, and that readers will return to these pages again and again for years to come—and every time discover new elements of the town's past.

In 1845 Ned Clemens (also known as "The Hermit of Old Orchard"), editor of the town's first newspaper *The Goose Fair Guide and Old Orchard Bellows*, predicted that the beach at Old Orchard would become world famous as a tourist center. Within a few years after his death, his prophesies began to come true.

By 1874 the destiny of Old Orchard literally came rolling into town. Three railroad stations provided summertime jump-off points for as many as ten thousand people a day attending camp meetings. Famous orators, such as Henry Cabot Lodge and Thomas B. Reed, spent time at the Beach, and the last of the bare-knuckle boxing champions, John L. Sullivan, visited nearly every Sunday for clambakes.

One year later, Ebenezer Staples, a town selectman, built the first of many elegant hotels in Old Orchard. The Old Orchard House, a three hundred-room resort, became synonymous with the town of Old Orchard and the elegant lifestyles of the most prestigious families of New England and Canada. Soon there were a dozen or more first-class hotels along the beach, where high-rise condominiums dominate the skyline today.

Originally a part of neighboring Saco, residents of "The Seashore at Saco" (as the area was known) felt they were being neglected by the mother town, and they grew tired of the poor treatment and elitist attitude shown them by the rest of Saco. After years of suffering fires without proper protection, disgruntled residents didn't need much more reason to seek relief from the state. Saco itself provided the final straw, according to Ernesto Brousseau, in a dispute over school textbooks in 1882. Disappointed with the politics of education, a school teacher by the name of Edgar Yates purchased books for his students with his own money. While this upset Saco officials, Staples, a town elder, took up Yates' cause and garnered 111 signatures on a petition which was presented to the state legislature. Shortly thereafter, on February 20, 1883, the town of Old Orchard was officially born.

In 1898 several families (including the Yates, Porter, Staples, and Milliken clans), as well as J.W. Duff, George Haley, and J.M. Ryan, banded together to form the Old Orchard Pier Company and build a huge steel pier into the ocean. The length of the original pier has long been in dispute: one source says the pier extended 1,787 feet into the Atlantic, while another source claims the structure was exactly 1,800 feet in length, and the town historian, Dan Blaney, says his best estimation is 1,823 feet. Regardless of the exact dimensions, the pier was symbolic of Old Orchard's increasing prosperity, but it would not remain so for long.

Fires played a major role in making and changing history in Old Orchard. In 1881, because of Saco's failure to provide adequate fire apparatus or protection, the seeds for secession were sewn. That year four major fires forced the area's residents to band together to purchase a fire bell and that effort also helped forge a bond of independence among Old Orchard residents that has carried through the years. On August 15, 1907, The Great Old Orchard Fire burned many of the larger hotels on the beach and charred more than one eighth of the town. Ruins were still smoldering in September of that year. It was said that the heat was so intense trains were forced to stop at the Atlantic and Walnut Street crossings because the rails were twisted from the heat of the fire. It was also reported that the blaze could be seen as far away as Sanford.

In an attempt to revive the summer tourist season, which had suffered from the loss of the great hotels, automobile racing was introduced to the hard-packed, low-tide sands of the beach. From 1911–14 races were held featuring the same style cars that were running in Indianapolis at the famed speedway, and drivers as famous as Barney Oldfield became a part of the racing scene here.

With the advent of air travel, Old Orchard became a favorite point of departure on transatlantic flights for famous pilots such as Frances Grayson, Clarence Chamberlain, and American hero Charles Lindbergh. Between the late 1920s and '30s, a number of transatlantic flights were attempted, and some were actually successful. Because of the long expanse of hard sand, the beach made an ideal runway for the mono-planes and bi-planes of the day. In fact, there was an airplane hanger at the beach where repairs and preparations could be made for flights of short and long distances.

This book is a look back at Old Orchard from the 1880s to the 1950s. Any historical research turns up numerous discrepancies in dates, times, size, and any number of other dimensions; this is not intended to be, nor is it possible to be, a definitive source for historical data. In its preparation, it became evident to me that what I have always speculated about history is true: it is not so much a matter of how things actually occurred but how people remember them. For every picture taken of a given event, there may be several different explanations for what was happening at that point. The photographs, moments frozen in time, may bring tears to the eyes of some of our cherished senior citizens; I hope they will give present current and future generations a chance to see where Old Orchard has been. Maybe, like "The Hermit of Old Orchard," someone will be able to see what lies ahead for Old Orchard Beach into the next century.

One

The Pier

"For years the dreams of an average Old Orchardite had been a pier," wrote the *Biddeford Journal* in 1898. "In vision he had feasted on the untold benefits which might accrue from a genuine substantial connection between land and water somewhere on the line of our splendid beach. Fleets of sailing and steam craft in the bay were pictured. Boating in all its vast variety: freight luggers and ocean steamers arriving and departing. Great crowds of promenaders taking in the sights and scenes from the pier deck while enterprising promoters of the scheme were coining a mint of hard dollars." (Ralph and Lois Duquette)

This photograph was taken in the spring of 1898, just prior to construction of the pier and shortly before the Cleaves Hotel (part of which can be seen in the background) was moved to the beach front to become Herbert L. Hildreth's Hotel Velvet. Nearly twenty years before the pier came into fruition, Winfield Dennett had proposed the construction of such a grand facility to enhance the town's tourist appeal and provide adequate docking for excursion boats and oceangoing vessels. However, it wasn't until the summer of 1895 that J.M. Ryan, a promoter from Detroit, arrived in Old Orchard and managed to persuade the town's fathers to form a corporation to lay plans for the first of many incarnations of the pier. A group of seven men, including Ryan, were initially responsible for the construction of the 1,823-foot-long structure. Stocks in the pier were sold and the Berlin Bridge Company of Berlin, New Hampshire, won the bid to build the landmark for a price of $38,000. (Ralph and Lois Duquette)

It took nearly two years to get the project off the ground and out into Saco Bay. Details were hammered out while public enthusiasm was gathered. But in 1897 a sudden shift in control over the project occurred. The "Velvet Molasses King," Herbert L. Hildreth, who was generally considered to be the driving force behind Old Orchard's acceptance as the "Coney Island" of the North, stepped in and offered the Old Orchard Pier Corporation his hotel lot as the shore side location of the pier. The corporation was all too happy to accept. Shortly thereafter, Hildreth proposed to buy a controlling interest in the company's stock. Hildreth not only knew the corporation was in desperate need of funding—they were unable to make a $10,000 payment on the first delivery of steel—but he felt the pier could be the premier attraction in all of Old Orchard. (Ralph and Lois Duquette)

Herbert L. Hildreth, the "Velvet Molasses King," started out as a plumber's helper as a child in Boston. Hildreth also worked as a photography salesman before entering the candy business. With limited success in Haverhill and Salem, Massachusetts, and Lewiston, Maine, he moved his confectionery business to Old Orchard where his peculiar combination of candy and photography was an instant success. In a short period of time he was able to purchase the Sears Bath Houses and again struck it rich with yet another odd combination, candy and public baths: records show he served thousands on weekend days during the summer. (Steve Fregeau)

Hildreth, entrepreneur, promoter, and the driving force behind the construction of the pier, bought the five-story gingerbread Cleaves Hotel and promptly moved it about one block to a location next to his bath houses. He then married all the buildings together to create the Hotel Velvet, named after one of his confectionery delights, the Velvet Molasses treat. The grandest hotel on the coast of New England, the Hotel Velvet (eventually re-named the Hotel Emerson) was complete with an elevator, electric lights, gigantic sun rooms, and a grand ballroom. It attracted the "hoi-pol loi" of the resorting society. Anyone who was anyone stayed at the Hotel Velvet. (Steve Fregeau)

In the winter of 1898 construction began on the largest steel pier in the entire world. Two hundred steel pilings were driven into the ledge offshore in one of the most ambitious land/sea projects ever undertaken on the Maine coast. In just four months, by June of 1898, the pier was finished. A 1898 advertising booklet boasted, "At last (after 20 years of failures) Old Orchard Beach Pier dreams have come true! The Old Orchard Pier, the finest and longest steel pier in the world, is built, and stands out in the ocean waves as a monument of the greatest engineering skills of pier building. There is a seating capacity of over 5,000 people. Boating, fishing and excursions can be had from the pier. Row and fishing boats to let, with experienced boatmen. A large parcel and bicycle check room at the cafe. Admission to pier 10 cents. No intoxicating liquors allowed on the pier. A force of policemen will patrol the pier to keep it free from disorderly persons." (Ralph and Lois Duquette)

Anticipation for the grand opening of the pier had grown to a fever pitch, due largely to the local papers that had been ballyhooing the event for months. Painchaud's Band was set up and ready to greet early morning arrivals to the tune of "The Only Real Thing on the Beach." Saco's mayor had declared that the pier would hold twenty thousand visitors at a time, which was about the combined populations of Old Orchard, Saco, and Biddeford, and that the pier would make Old Orchard the Coney Island of New England. It was one of the grandest events ever on the coast of Maine, as bands played, flags were unfurled, and thousands of visitors paid $10 a piece to be among the first on Herbert Hildreth's Golden Mile. One of the most peculiar facts about the pier is that it extended so far into the ocean that it was actually a part of Saco, and the town of Old Orchard did not enjoy any tax dollars from the business at the end of the pier. Saco was responsible for policing the end of the structure. (Steve Fregeau)

Three large pavilions, a casino, a bandstand, and a cafe occupied the ultimate location at the end of the pier. On the day of the grand opening, July 2, 1898, the faithful were treated to concerts, speeches, and one of the biggest fireworks displays of the time. Later, some enterprising people installed a miniature open-air locomotive to take passengers from one end of the pier to the other. The fare was just a nickel; many perspective "gay-blades" and their partners rode out to the dance pavilion to save their energies for the festivities of the evening. (Ralph and Lois Duquette)

Five months later, the pier was fighting for its life. One of H.L. Hildreth's partners, J.W. Duff, described what occurred at around 3 a.m. on December 4, 1898, like this: "Wreckage from the schooner, *Grecian Bend*, was the entering wedge which led to the collapse of the pier. The floating planks, together with the force of the wind and waves, succeeded in demolishing the V-shaped wooden breakwater at the extreme end of the pier. Then the wreckage began to pound at the trestle work underneath and soon tore them from their fastenings. The building (pavilion) at the end of the pier was ripped away suddenly with a deafening crash. It was carried away toward Bay View and soon grounded on the surf in front of the Atlantic House." (Ralph and Lois Duquette)

18

The storm also severed connections with a popular summertime experience enjoyed by many. According to the *Biddeford Journal*, "The excursion steamer, the *Pilgrim*, used to put into the Casino end of the pier, puffing gently on her sonorous whistle and dispensing passengers-cum-dancers. Later that night, she would put to sea again for a languid return to the port of Portland, with knots of exhausted dancers sprinkled around her ample decks." (Ralph and Lois Duquette)

For most of the century following the storm of December 4, 1898, bits and pieces of the pier have washed up on shore, a reminder of what Mother Nature has in store for man-made wonders. Over the course of the next ninety years, various other piers have appeared on the beach at Old Orchard; like their predecessors, all eventually succumbed to the ravages of time, saltwater, storms, and fire. Today's current installment, roughly 400 feet in length, is a mere quarter of the original and is awaiting the day when Mother Nature comes calling again. (Steve Fregeau)

During the harsh winter months in Old Orchard, the weather does battle with man-made structures, and the structures don't always win. In 1978, a storm similar to this one finally claimed the building at the end of the pier: strong winds combined with enormous waves and crashed through the sea side of the Casino, flooding it with saltwater. At the time that the waves broke through the ocean end of the structure, the doors and windows at the front were blown out. For months after, debris, furnishings, and arcade games washed up on shore. (Ralph and Lois Duquette)

"I met my wife-to-be at the Casino," said Warren Harmon in an interview with the *Biddeford Journal* in March of 1970. "So many people got to dancing, it made you dizzy. The orchestra had to change the beat sometimes to a slower one when the dance floor started to rock like a boat in a storm."

On August 15, 1907, the Hotel Emerson (formerly the Velvet) burned to the ground, and in its wake, the fire claimed the first 100 feet of the pier. Several hundred people were reported to have been trapped on the pier when the fire began and quick thinking saved many lives. Many of the men trapped on the pier began tearing up the planks of wood that made the boardwalk, thus separating themselves from the fire. The sagging steel support beams of the pier are

testimony to the intensity of the fire. The trains seen here are taking thousands of Bostonians back to Beantown with only the clothes they were wearing. The chimney on the right is from the Hotel Emerson. The town hall can be seen here in the center of the photograph. (Ralph and Lois Duquette)

The entrance to the pier as it looked shortly after it opened on July 3, 1898. (Ralph and Lois Duquette)

"Free Dancing Lessons," reads the sign in the middle of this picture. "Every Morning. 10-11. Private Lessons by Appointment." Dancing was one of the biggest draws to the Casino at the end of the pier. Here the Jack Rabbit Rollercoaster and the Old Orchard House can be seen in the background. These two structures, along with the pier itself, were for generations probably the three most recognizable landmarks in Old Orchard. (Old Orchard Beach Historical Society)

(Old Orchard Beach Historical Society)

The pier train was the smallest steam locomotive in the world. Each car carried one passenger and the entire length of the trip was from one end of the pier to the other. Built in 1899, the pier train was constructed the year following the opening of the pier. Like the Dummy, the pier train had no provisions for turning around. When it reached its destination, it would back up to the origination point at the opposite end of the pier. Ten cents would buy a round-trip ticket. (Old Orchard Beach Historical Society)

Night and day. These photographs show the same location, at the entrance to the pier. Even though these pictures appear to be nearly the same, there are some subtle differences between them, reflecting the ever-changing face of Old Orchard. (Old Orchard Beach Historical Society)

(Old Orchard Beach Historical Society)

Not only was the shoreline constantly changing, but the pier itself received several face-lifts over a short span of time. The top photograph was taken shortly after the fire of 1907; the bottom one was taken just a few years later around 1915. (Old Orchard Beach Historical Society)

What was left of the pier following the February 1978 storm. The entire pier was so weakened by this storm that trucks were not be allowed to drive down the pier to aid in the cleanup. Debris had to be hauled away by helicopter. (Ralph and Lois Duquette)

Two

A Place to Stay

The square at the turn of the twentieth century. Two of Old Orchard's most famous hotels, the Alberta (on the left) and the Hotel Velvet (on the right) can be seen here. Today, one can only imagine what a center of commerce and hospitality this town was. (Steve Fregeau)

The Hotel Fiske. One of the beach front's most prominent hotels, the Fiske was a favorite among Old Orchard's wealthier visitors. Many of the Hotel Fiske's clientele were annual guests and many friendships developed over the years. In 1901, "Town Topics," a column in the *Old Orchard Mirror* stated: "Austin H. Fiske will have the management of the Hotel Fiske this season, and you may depend upon it that this well-known and popular hostelry will not only have the high standard that it has already reached, maintained in every respect, but it would not be the least bit surprising if Austin added to the efficiency of the house, if such a thing is possible. But at any rate, you may rest assured that the Hotel Fiske will be one of the most carefully managed hotels on the Maine coast, and that is saying a little bit." (Steve Fregeau)

The Hotel Velvet. The gingerbread architecture of this majestic five-story building made it the most distinctive hotel on the beach. The Velvet was at the head of the square, and served as the gateway to the pier. It was the Velvet's owner, H.L. Hildreth, who provided the land and much of the financing for the construction of the pier in 1898. The Velvet was originally part of the Cleaves Hotel and was located across the railroad tracks, a block or so from the beach front. (Steve Fregeau)

H.L. Hildreth, the "Velvet Molasses King," made his original fortune from selling confectionery delights in Massachusetts. Eventually he made his way to Old Orchard and combined his candy-making skills with, first a photography studio, and then a bath house. It is supposed that all of Hildreth's photographs were burned in the fire of 1907. Shortly before that great fire, Hildreth sold his interest in the hotel and it was re-named the Hotel Emerson. (Steve Fregeau)

The Vermont. (Steve Fregeau)

The Alcazar, also known as the Palace Hotel. (Steve Fregeau)

The Seashore House. (Steve Fregeau)

The Bernard House. (Steve Fregeau)

The Forest Pier Hotel (and Egyptian Bazaar). (Steve Fregeau)

The Irving. (Steve Fregeau)

The New Palmer House. (Steve Fregeau)

The Aldine Hotel. An advertisement for this hotel appeared in the *Old Orchard Mirror* and claimed that the Aldine could accommodate 150 guests. It also stated that the Aldine ". . . commands a most charming view of ocean and country. Its rooms are bright and airy. Lighted by gas, each room also features electric call bells and spring water runs throughout the house. The sanitary conditions are perfect and well arranged. In the rear is a fine grove, extensive lawns and broad piazzas surround the house. An orchestra is on hand to play for dancing during the season. Mr. S. Haynes, the general proprietor, has the pleasure of seeing his former guests return to again enjoy the hospitality of the house." (Ralph and Lois Duquette)

The new Old Orchard House on Old Orchard Street. (Ralph and Lois Duquette)

Built by Ebenezer C. Staples, "the most cantankerous S.O.B. this town has ever known," the Old Orchard House was the granddaddy of all Old Orchard hotels, and was the first truly grand hotel. Perched high on a hill near Saco Avenue, looking toward the beach, the Old Orchard House had over three hundred rooms and a boardwalk that stretched for hundreds of yards nearly all the way to the beach. Although the Old Orchard House escaped the Great Fire of 1907 it couldn't elude the wrecking ball; having grown into disrepair, it was torn down in 1943. (Old Orchard Beach Historical Society)

The Old Orchard House. (Old Orchard Beach Historical Society)

Three

The Great
Old Orchard Fire

It was the height of the wildest summer season the town had ever seen. Old Orchard had not ever been as crowded as it was on August 15, 1907. The Boston and Maine Railroad had run a special excursion rate of $2 for a trip from North Station in Boston to Old Orchard. Every hotel, every rooming house, and all of the campgrounds were full and the overflow was forced to seek refuge in Portland and surrounding communities. Those people were among the fortunate. (Steve Fregeau)

The remains of the Olympia. It is believed that this was the site where the most devastating fire in Old Orchard history began. At around 7:55 on the evening of August 15, it was reported that a fire had broken out in one of the buildings of the Hotel Alberta about a block from the pier at the center of the beach. The Olympia was a connecting building where members of the summer staff were housed, and it is widely believed that the first smoke and flames were seen coming out of the window of a room where a young women may have accidently knocked over a lamp, igniting the spilled oil with a curling iron and catching the curtains on fire. A contemporary newspaper recounted a possible origin of the fire: "It was widely reported by several 'street corner Johnnies' who practised the fine art of 'girl watching' that they saw a young girl in the help's quarters of the Hotel Alberta knock over a lamp, and within seconds, the curtains were ablaze." (Steve Fregeau)

It didn't take long for the entire Hotel Emerson, a five-story structure made completely of wood (kindling, more precisely), to burn to the ground. In a matter of eighteen minutes the structure was destroyed. Because of the proximity of the pier to the Hotel Emerson, the partly-wooden structure caught fire as well, trapping hundreds who sought refuge on the walkway. (Steve Fregeau)

Old Orchard Beach the day after the fire. The ruins were still smoldering when the curious came out in search of personal belongings, or just to discuss the tragedy. This shot looks back from the beach toward the train station. From the oceanfront to the train station and for several blocks both ways the Great Old Orchard Fire wiped out nearly one eighth of the town. The Old Orchard House can be seen in the background. It was one of the only hotels left in town. (Steve Fregeau)

RUINS AT OLD ORCHARD BEACH
COPYRIGHTED 1907 BY
HANSON - PORTLAND ME.

One of the more famous spectators of the Great Old Orchard Fire was the mayor of Boston John "Honey Fitz" Fitzgerald, father of Rose Fitzgerald—who just that summer had become engaged to Joseph Kennedy in the social event of the season (Joseph would be the grandfather of President John F. Kennedy). Fitzgerald felt it was his duty to take charge of the emergency and telephoned the Portland Police. "Send us your engines and policemen. The looting of property is dreadful. They are taking trunks from the burning buildings and breaking them open in the streets." In response, the police and fire equipment were sent by fast train with the throttle open and fastened down; the safety valves blowing steam and the whistle shrieking as the train hurtled through the night.

The problem of looting certainly took its toll on the visitors. The *Portland Evening Express* reported that the "... stunned vacationers had to protect their possessions while 'the sparks fell so thickly that screams of pain and curses were often heard as the hot brands fell upon the flesh of the refugees.'" But according to more than a few eyewitnesses, Fitzgerald was more of a hindrance than a help. "Most old timers admit that there was a heated discussion between Fitz and the Old Orchard Fire Chief to the effect that if he (Fitzgerald) didn't stop meddlin' he'd get a hose turned on him and rolled back across the lawn of the Old Orchard House." (Steve Fregeau)

The loss was nearly total. The fire consumed everything in its path. Since most of the structures were made of wood, it didn't take long for seventeen hotels, sixty cottages, and scores of other buildings to be wiped out. Even though the most destructive fire in the history of Old Orchard caused more than a million and a half (1907) dollars damage to property, it could have been worse. Only three people were directly killed by the tragic events of August 15, 1907. The *Portland Evening Express* reported, ". . . As the flames reached Hogan's Drug Store, someone yelled that there was a can of gasoline inside. A young spectator immediately raced into the burning building and carried it out. But just as he reached the street with his volatile cargo, there was a violent explosion from inside the store as a soda tank exploded. One man was decapitated by the flying steel. Two others received such serious injuries they died 2 days later, never having regained consciousness." Just one month earlier, a fire similarly destroyed much of Coney Island in New York. It was a disastrous summer for the amusement business. (Steve Fregeau)

The end of the pier. This photograph was taken on August 16, 1907. Made of steel and wood and constructed in 1898, it would take much more than a fire to wipe out this historic Old Orchard landmark. "The embers of the great fire are not yet cool, the day after the blaze," said the *Daily Eastern Argus*, "and already the solid men of the town are getting together and figuring what they will do to promote the best interests of the community. The impression has gone out that the town is wiped out utterly destroyed beyond hope of redemption. As a matter of fact only about one eighth of it in area has been burned over and while it is a fact that almost all of the larger hotels have been burned it is also a fact that there are a multitude of smaller places, cottages and other similar institutions which are as ready for business as they ever were. Old Orchard today can accommodate a lot of people." The *Argus* continued: "It is thought, that about three hotels will take the place of the host of small ones destroyed and that the beach will be the net gainer in the end. It is no secret that an awful lot of trash was wiped out in the fire. The wiping out of which will undoubtedly benefit the community as a whole." (Steve Fregeau)

A large percentage of the victims of the fire spent the bone-chilling night sleeping on the beach on mattresses that had been rescued from the burning hotels and cottages. During the heat of the blaze, summer tourists and residents, hotel owners and their staffs, and bystanders and onlookers were kept busy carrying out furnishings, belongings, and fixtures from the hotels and cottages. The fire occurred at low tide, providing a wide expanse of beach for the mountains of furniture and personal belongings. But as the fire raged on, the tide swept in and captured much of what was stored on the beach, doubling the tragic effects of the fire. (Steve Fregeau)

Theodore W. Mingo, then a volunteer torch bearer for the Old Orchard Fire Department, later remembered the fire: "The Hotel Velvet (called the Hotel Emerson at the time of the fire), which was five stories tall, was made completely of wood and burned to the ground in just eighteen minutes." Mingo later became chief of the fire department and retired from duty in 1957. (Steve Fregeau)

The devastation was severe—not even a hurricane could cause this type of damage to Old Orchard. Most of the buildings consumed in the Great Old Orchard Fire of 1907 were never rebuilt. (Steve Fregeau)

47

The Hotel Fiske. Within a short period of time, the Fiske, which was a block or so away from the source of the fire, was consumed. Note the men in the water in the foreground. Another reason the 1907 fire was so devastating was the strong wind which fanned the flames and helped the fire spread for blocks. It is said that residents of Prout's Neck in neighboring Scarborough were hosing down their houses in case the fire swept down the beach. Fire companies from Saco, Biddeford, and Portland were called to the blaze but none of their equipment fit the hydrants in Old Orchard. At the time of the fire, the Old Orchard Fire Department was limited to one horse-drawn engine and one horse cart. Inadequate water pressure kept firefighters from reaching any higher than the first three stories of any of the buildings. By the time the Portland fire company could muster and make its way to Old Orchard, an hour and a half had elapsed. Even if the Portland equipment had arrived at the conflagration sooner, it couldn't have gotten anywhere near the blaze because the railroad tracks had been warped by the intense heat of the fire. It was reported in the Portland papers that a "curious glow appeared on the Southern horizon that could be seen from the [Portland's] Eastern Promenade." Other accounts said the smoke and fire could be see from as far away as Sanford. (Steve Fregeau)

What's left of the Alberta, Emerson (Velvet), Fiske, New Palmer, and other hotels. The only parts of these elegant hotels that were fireproof were the chimneys. It is ironic that advertisements for the Hotel Velvet made strong mention of the hotel's fire-resistance properties, with one stating that it was perfectly safe for its guests. Yet despite the total destruction of the building, there was not a single fatality at the site and not one guest reported so much as a scrape. Three people lost their lives in the town during the fire and one more, an elderly gentleman, died a few days later from a heart attack suffered during the height of the blaze. (Steve Fregeau)

From the beach, the end of the pier acted like a wick on a very long candle. About the first 100 feet of the pier were consumed by the fire. (Steve Fregeau)

Four

The Square

A gathering place, a parking place, a place for amusement: the square has always been at the center of the action in Old Orchard. (Old Orchard Beach Historical Society)

Amusements of all types were available to tourists in the square. Here, two small model planes travel on a near collision course to the delight of spectators. The sparks were all part of the show.

This photograph, taken from a postcard made shortly after the Great Old Orchard Fire of 1907, leaves little doubt as to the main attraction of Old Orchard. The Forest Pier Hotel building was also host to "Pier Drug Store" and the "Pier Dairy" lunch counter. (Steve Fregeau)

This photograph was taken at the same location as the one above but from a slightly different angle and a few years later. One thing that has always been constant in Old Orchard, even today, is that everything is subject to change. Look closely and you will see that a local real estate company was selling house lots in Old Orchard for $29.99. (Steve Fregeau)

The hustle and bustle of the square. It looks here like "cruising" was a favorite pastime, even in 1922. (Old Orchard Beach Historical Society)

A rare quiet moment on a summer day in the late 1950s. (Old Orchard Beach Historical Society)

Memorial Day, 1953. There are more people in this photograph than lived year-round in the entire town in that year. This picture is looking from the head of the square up toward Saco Avenue. (Old Orchard Beach Historical Society)

"Try a real ride," challenges a sign on the Jack and Jill Slide (on the left) in this 1940s photograph. The Jack Rabbit Rollercoaster is on the right.

Five

The Beach

Some of the staff of the Old Orchard House, which can be seen here in the background. There was a boardwalk from the grand hotel that extended almost to the beach. Also in this picture is the Sea Shore Public Bath House. Bath houses were a big business in Old Orchard from the mid-1800s until after the turn of the century. (Old Orchard Beach Historical Society)

Googin's Rocks at low tide, looking toward the pier. The only thing that ever changes on the beach are the fashions.

Peanuts, popcorn, and crackerjack on the beach at Old Orchard. As warm as the weather must have been in summers past, rarely did beachgoers expose too much to the sun and heat. (Ralph and Lois Duquette)

The Peanutine wagon, from a famous postcard of the 1890s. This young lad was one of the most photographed persons on the beach. His mule team helped him sell a peanut confection up and down the beach. (Steve Fregeau)

Googin's Rocks was and still is a popular "nesting" spot for beachgoers. At high tide, of course, this perch is completely underwater.

Old Orchard Beach before the pier was built. On the left side of this photograph can be seen a sign for Hildreth's Bath House Pavilion. It is supposed that this shot was taken 1897, just before construction of the pier was begun. It also was apparently before Hildreth moved the Cleaves Hotel to the beach. (Steve Fregeau)

A bathing beauty poses in front of the pier. (Nanci Boutet and Ruth Goodale Boutet)

This photograph is a cornucopia of what the beach meant to visitors. Note the man at left on a surfboard and the crowd gathering for an unknown reason. Also, there is a man carrying a

sign: he is either protesting or selling something. (Ralph and Lois Duquette)

Business as usual. Right along the northern side of the pier, one could buy picture postcards, tintypes, and peanuts, or visit the Merry Widow Pavilion. Long dresses, wool suits, and parasols were the order of the day for the beach. (Steve Fregeau)

A family reunion of sorts on the beach around the beginning of the twentieth century. Many families have been coming to Old Orchard for generations. (Old Orchard Beach Historical Society)

A typical beach day of the 1940s—not much different from today. (Old Orchard Beach Historical Society)

(Old Orchard Beach Historical Society)

Six

Planes, Trains, and Automobiles

Old Orchard and Maine's first man of the air, Harry M. Jones, was as much a showman and promoter as he was a top-flight pilot and airman.

Harry M. Jones and his Curtiss JN-4C Canuck, ready for business. On August 11, 1921, the town of Old Orchard made the beach an official runway for air planes and heavier-than-air craft. By 1933, Harry M. Jones was appointed by Governor Louis Brann to be Maine's first airport supervisor. Jones designed twenty-one of Maine's first airports, and eighteen of them were built by the WPA. (Leo Boyle, Maine Aviation Historical Society)

Ever the promoter, Harry Jones advertises the price of a pair of shoes for the Hazzard Shoe Company. Mr. Robert Hazzard, a financial backer, owned a shoe company in Gardiner and had a summer cottage near the Scarborough town line. Hazzard put up the money for Jones' hangar and first plane. Upon further inspection of this photograph, one can see Jones waving to the camera on the starboard side of the plane. (Leo Boyle, Maine Aviation Historical Society)

According to Leo Boyle, president of the Maine Aviation Historical Society, Harry Jones convinced the governor of Maine to appoint him to the position of the first aerial policeman in the state. Although his duties were negligible and mostly ceremonial, it was another of Jones' self-promotional tricks that earned him a lot of attention and added to his reputation as one of America's premier aviators. (Leo Boyle, Maine Aviation Historical Society)

Pilot Harry Jones poses as "another" famous aviator. Here, Jones stands on the strut of his Stinson SB-1B Detroiter on December 21, 1937, ready to drop gifts to needy children in Portland. (Leo Boyle, Maine Aviation Historical Society)

70

Harry Jones was the perfect man for the job. An excellent pilot and airman, he began his flying career as a passenger on a flight in 1911, just eight years after the Wright Brothers flew at Kitty Hawk. The owner of the Hazzard Shoe Company put up the money for Jones' hangar and flight school in exchange for some of the most unique advertising of the day. Before Lindbergh's famous flight, Harry M. Jones was already flying thousands of tourists from his air strip on the beach near the Scarborough town line to Portland and back for as much as $25 for two passengers. On January 2, 1913, Jones became the first and last pilot to land a plane on the Boston Commons. The Boston newspaper, *The Post*, ran a contest in 1912 that would pay the first aviator to land on the Commons $10,000. After an earlier attempt in bad weather and an accident, Jones made his landing but two days too late to claim the prize. *The Post* backed out of their offer on the technicality and Jones was subsequently arrested for landing his plane there. (Leo Boyle, Maine Aviation Historical Society)

This photograph was taken on June 13, 1929, and is very interesting because in addition to Harry M. Jones' plane on the left (in the foreground), the other planes in this shot include, from left to right: a Ballanca J *Green Flash*; John Domenjoz' sailing glider (now restored at the Owl's Head Transportation Museum); and *Yellowbird*, a Bernard 191. Later on this day the *Green Flash* would crash on takeoff at the beach in an attempt to fly nonstop across the Atlantic, while *Yellowbird*, complete with a 10-inch Florida alligator as a mascot, made it from Old Orchard to the coast of Spain. (Leo Boyle, Maine Aviation Historical Society)

Charles Lindbergh (center) and Harry Jones (right) at the Hazzard Shoe Flying Corporation's hangar. Only thirty-seven days after Lindbergh returned to the United States from France, he landed *The Spirit of St. Louis* on the beach at Old Orchard. The plane, built for a paltry $15,000, now hangs at the Smithsonian Institute in Washington, DC. A replica of *The Spirit of St. Louis* landed in a ceremony at the beach in 1977, commemorating the fiftieth anniversary of the flight. (Leo Boyle, Maine Aviation Historical Society)

Charles Lindbergh alongside *The Spirit of St. Louis.* (Leo Boyle, Maine Aviation Historical Society)

Lindbergh in Old Orchard. According to Leo Boyle, Lindbergh flew his entire tour around America wearing a full suit to prove to Americans how easy and uncomplicated air flight was. Fifty years after Lindbergh's historic flight and subsequent appearance in Old Orchard a commemorative "fly-in" was held to celebrate the anniversary. Lindbergh's widow Anne was invited to participate in the festivities but sent a letter of apology instead. Part of her letter read: ". . . I am well aware of the importance of Old Orchard Beach in the history of Transatlantic flying and in my husband's life. On our early flying trips to Maine, after our marriage, he went out of his way to pass over your famous beach and show it to me. I know it stirred many memories in him, not only of his own "unscheduled" landing but of the many historic and fateful take-offs of that early era. I felt he wanted to pay tribute to the pioneers who left that strip of land for an unknown destiny, many of them not to return—others to gain victory and acclaim . . ." (Leo Boyle, Maine Aviation Historical Society and Libby Memorial Library)

Aviation legend Igor Sikorsky (left) and Harry Jones. Many famous pilots landed at Old Orchard Beach. Such famous aviation pioneers as Sikorsky, Clarence Campbell, Bill Boeing, and Donald Douglas, along with Charles Lindbergh and Wiley Post, used the sandy runway at the beach. Sikorsky, who was born in Kiev, Russia, and had designed a bomber-type aircraft for his country, eventually immigrated to the United States where he set up an aircraft manufacturing business located in New York. (Leo Boyle, Maine Aviation Historical Society)

Wiley Post and Harold Gatty on a stop during a barnstorming tour in Old Orchard. The pair were the first to fly completely around the world in their plane, the *Winnie Mae*. This picture was taken in 1935. Post later flew entirely around the world solo in 1933. On August 16, 1935, shortly after this photograph was taken, Post and American treasure and humorist, Will Rogers, perished in a plane crash in northern Alaska. (Leo Boyle, Maine Aviation Historical Society)

Wiley Post and Harold Gatty relaxing at the beach at Old Orchard. In August 1931, the *Portland Evening Express* told of the preparations for the arrival of Post and Gatty: "Arrangements have been made for the famous around the world flyers, Wiley Post and Harold Gatty, to be guests of the Old Orchard Beach (American Legion) post Thursday, August 13. They are expected to arrive at about 10 o'clock in the morning and their plane, the *Winnie Mae*, will be stationed in the square at the foot of Old Orchard street all through the day. The Palace ballroom has been engaged and Miss Carmela Ponselle, distinguished mezzo-soprano, will sing the national anthem in honor of the world flyers. Miss Ponselle, who is spending the summer at her log cabin in Fern Park will be a great drawing card, as her beautiful voice has greatly charmed all who have heard her sing. Another special feature will be the presence of nine American beauties, including Miss America, Miss France, etc., who will come from New York to select Miss Old Orchard Beach of 1931 . . . A big banquet will be given in honor of the flyers at the Hotel Vesper at 10 o'clock Thursday evening." (Leo Boyle, Maine Aviation Historical Society and the Old Orchard Beach Historical Society)

A *c.* 1931 photograph of Wiley Post, Harold Gatty, and the commander of American Legion Post #57, Carl Davis.

The *Columbia*. This plane was one of the largest to ever land at Old Orchard, and could carry as many as twenty to twenty-five passengers at a time. (Leo Boyle, Maine Aviation Historical Society)

John Domenjoz had a vision of a unique style of glider. Incredible as it may seem, Domenjoz believed that once his aircraft was in flight, the sail atop the wings would actually work like a sailboat, catching the wind and helping to keep him aloft. This plane was invented in 1929 but was soon dismantled and kept in two crates until it was restored in 1964 and moved to the Owl's Head Transportation Museum, where it is on display today. From left to right in this photograph are Harry Jones, Ira "Joe" Snow (mechanic), and John Domenjoz (in the cockpit). (Leo Boyle, Maine Aviation Historical Society)

The *Dawn*, seen here on the beach at night. It was a full moon, and an imposing storm at high tide nearly destroyed the *Dawn*. Note the flags of Denmark and the United States on the tail assembly. Its owners, Mrs. Frances Wilson Grayson (of Arkansas and then New York) and Mrs. Ange Ancker (of Denmark), formed the Ancker-Grayson Flying Corporation. Together they paid Igor Sikorsky, who taught Mrs. Grayson to fly, $40,000 for the *Dawn*, which they hoped could fly Grayson to Copenhagen, Denmark, in an effort to become the first woman to fly across the Atlantic. (Leo Boyle, Maine Aviation Historical Society)

Disaster followed the *Dawn* at nearly every turn. Even before the *Dawn* could take off from Old Orchard, it was caught in a ferocious Nor'easter and nearly washed out to sea. (Leo Boyle, Maine Aviation Historical Society)

Harry M. Jones and Mrs. Frances Grayson, a real estate mogul from New York. When the *Dawn* was about 500 miles into its first attempt at a transatlantic flight, the plane developed engine trouble; the pilot, Wilmer Stultz, eventually persuaded Grayson to allow them to turn around and return to America to make repairs. Undocumented reports say that Grayson, unwilling to give up her quest to become the first female to fly the Atlantic, pulled a gun on Stultz to try to persuade him to continue. Stultz and logic eventually won out and they barely made it back to the mainland, on just one engine. In a second attempt late in December 1927, Grayson and a Norwegian pilot, Oskar Omdal, who was familiar with arctic flying, took off in the *Dawn* from Roosevelt Field in New York. Their course would have brought the plane very close to Old Orchard, Newfoundland, and then England or France before the final destination of Denmark, but they disappeared en route and were never heard from again. In 1928 a message in a bottle washed up on shore at Salem, Massachusetts, that read: "1928. We are freezing. Gas leaked and we are drifting off Grand Bank. Grayson." It was never determined if that message was actually written by Grayson, but no one has ever found the remains of the plane or its occupants. (Leo Boyle, Maine Aviation Historical Society)

The crew and some on lookers check the damage to the *Green Flash*, which crashed trying to take off from the beach on June 13, 1929. While attempting to gain speed for lift-off, the plane hit a sink hole in the beach and caused major damage to the front of the plane, including the propeller. (Leo Boyle, Maine Aviation Historical Society)

Yellowbird and the *Green Flash* on the morning both planes were to attempt a transatlantic crossing. Only the French plane, *Yellowbird*, was successful on this day; later, the *Green Flash*, after making some repairs, would make the crossing as well. Ironically, both planes had to put down short of their destination of Paris and Rome, respectively, on the same beach, 5 miles apart, in Spain. *Yellowbird* refueled and then flew on to Mimezan, France, now the sister city of Old Orchard. (Leo Boyle, Maine Aviation Historical Society)

The *Pathfinder* fueling up for an attempt to cross the Atlantic. Fuel was strained through a chamois cloth before being put into the plane. Because there were no actual gas pumps, planes actually had to siphon the gas from the barrels in the foreground. (Leo Boyle, Maine Aviation Historical Society)

OOD FOR ONE AIRPLANE RID

575

2nd Annual Aviation Meet
Old Orchard, Maine
August 29, 30, 31, September 1, 1924
Auspices C. Fayette Staples Post 57
Dept. of Maine, American Legion
*This ticket good any time this year
with Capt. Harry M. Jones, A.S., O.R.C.*

(Leo Boyle, Maine Aviation Historical Society)

Yellowbird being readied for take off. One of the strangest stories of an early transatlantic crossing concerns this French plane and a stowaway. Pilot Armen Lotti, Jr., along with crewmen Jean Assolant and Rene Lefevre, decided to fly their mono-plane from Old Orchard to Paris on June 13, 1929. Their plane was prepared for the long distance flight at the Hazzard Shoe Flying Corporation's hangar (the present-day site of the Friendship Motel), and had to be moved from the hangar to the sandy runway. Twenty-two-year-old Portland native Arthur Schreiber was at the beach, and on a dare attempted to hitch a ride on *Yellowbird*. When he asked Lotti, the plane's owner, if there was room, he was coldly told no. But when Lotti and his crew needed volunteers to push the plane on to the beach, there was Schreiber at the ready. As Schreiber pushed from the back of the plane, a hatch at the rear opened and he saw his chance. He quickly climbed in and hid in the rear compartment of the plane, where he remained silent until the plane was nearly an hour off the shore, and then presented himself to the crew. "I felt like throwing him overboard," said Assolant. "We felt such a wave of anger that we were on the point of beating him. We felt that he had not only jeopardized our elaborate plans but had even imperiled our lives," said Lefevre. Eventually, Lotti and his crew accepted him as cargo and ordered him to fill four cups of cognac after which they toasted Schreiber and his daring. No one is certain if the extra 120 pounds Schreiber added to the plane was responsible for it not making its final destination of Paris, or if it was the poor weather conditions on the last five hours that caused the quartet to set down on the northern coast of Spain. It is quite possible that when this photograph was taken, Schreiber was making his move into the back of the plane. (Leo Boyle, Maine Aviation Historical Society)

The Pride of Detroit. On August 26, 1929, *The Pride of Detroit* left Old Orchard Beach on an "around-the-world" flight attempt, but after successfully navigating from North America to England and then on to Tokyo, the final leg of the flight was scrubbed. According to Leo Boyle, there was such public outcry when *The Pride of Detroit* made it to Japan, they stopped their attempt. Many felt that because of all the tragic endings to transatlantic attempts, a transpacific flight was too dangerous. (Leo Boyle, Maine Aviation Historical Society)

A bathing beauty on the beach in 1922 in front of Harry M. Jones' hangar. (Leo Boyle, Maine Aviation Historical Society)

Old Glory. Upon takeoff, this plane would be carrying 1,179 gallons of fuel and a combined weight of nearly 13,000 pounds. In his book, *Flight Fever* (1971), Joseph Hamlin wrote: "Suddenly, she was off—only a little, yet off, but the pier was closing in on her fast. She'd never clear it! At the last minute, we saw one golden wing dip as Hill (the pilot) banked gingerly around the edge of the dance pavilion and open air movie at the end, still only twenty feet in the air. As she flew out over the Saco coast toward Biddeford Pool, she gained little or no altitude. We could see her struggling. We held our breaths. As she neared Wood Island Light on Fortunes Rocks, *Old Glory* began to climb. Harry Jones, who followed them in his plane, said that a puff of air had sprung up from the southeast just at the right moment and had helped lift her to a safer 500 feet. We watched her, spellbound, as she banked gently over Biddeford Pool and headed to the northeast . . ." (Leo Boyle, Maine Aviation Historical Society)

Old Glory gets a police escort down the beach from twelve motorcycle policemen. It didn't help. *Old Glory* crashed, with no survivors. (Leo Boyle, Maine Aviation Historical Society)

Another photograph of *Old Glory*, which was owned by William Randolph Hearst. Here, the crew of J.D. Hill, Phillip Payne (the general manager of the *New York Daily Mirror*), unknown, and Lloyd Bertaud (pilot), are shown at Old Orchard before their doomed flight. Fourteen hours after takeoff, an S.O.S. signal was picked up by the SS *Transylvania* but the crew-less wreckage was not picked up until several days later. (Leo Boyle, Maine Aviation Historical Society)

Harry M. Jones' plane at the head of the square in Old Orchard. Even though airplanes on the beach became commonplace, Jones' planes, as well as the countless others, always drew a crowd. (Leo Boyle, Maine Aviation Historical Society)

Harry M. Jones' plane on the beach just south of the pier. A *Portland Sunday Telegram* article written in 1924 stated: "Not the least of the sporting advantages (at Old Orchard) is the air service. Airplanes are ever ready to take their patrons for an airing above the beach and surf and thousands avail themselves of this opportunity each year. Wonderful natural flying field for aviators is bringing new fame to the beach." (Leo Boyle, Maine Aviation Historical Society)

The first known aerial view of Old Orchard Beach. Even though this photograph was taken in 1912, only about half of the original pier can be seen here: storms wiped out much of the end of the pier in 1898. Just north and to the left of the pier one can see the Kite Track, a harness racing track in Old Orchard that operated from the late nineteenth century until just before this photograph was taken. It was reopened in the 1930s and races were held for four weeks every summer until July 3, 1950. (Leo Boyle, Maine Aviation Historical Society)

One of the first known photographs of an airplane over the beach at Old Orchard. (Leo Boyle, Maine Aviation Historical Society)

A squadron of World War I bombers in a fly-over at an air show in 1922. (Old Orchard Beach Historical Society)

The crew of the *Roma*. (Leo Boyle, Maine Aviation Historical Society)

The *Pathfinder*. (Leo Boyle, Maine Aviation Historical Society)

Take a Flight Over Portlar

I will carry passengers, two at a time, from Old Orchar
Portland and back via Old Orchard Beach, Prouts Neck and $
boro Beach. The charge will be $25.00 for two passengers, and
round trip will take about twenty minutes. When flying over the
I will rise to a height of 4,200 feet, which will be high enough to a
gliding to a convenient landing place should it be necessary to r
a landing.

Over4,300 pasengers carried safely since taking up aviation
never an accident of any kind.

HARRY M. JONES, Aviator

(Leo Boyle, Maine Aviation Historic Society)

Of course, the railroads played a large part in making Old Orchard a popular summertime resort spot in the Northeast. Not only did the trains bring vacationers, often times entire families for the whole summer, to the grand hotels and family cottages, but the religious faithful by the tens of thousands also came pouring into Old Orchard and Ocean Park on a daily basis. Oh, and the occasional president would stop by: here, Teddy Roosevelt whistlestops through Old Orchard on the campaign trail. (Ralph and Lois Duquette)

Two trains which serviced Old Orchard over the years were known as The Flying Yankee. Both were owned by the Boston and Maine Railroad, and they carried passengers to and from Boston and points south all summer long. (Steve Fregeau)

The Dummy Railroad was a 3.24 mile stretch of the Boston and Maine Railroad with stations in Old Orchard, Ocean Park, and Camp Ellis. It began on June 26, 1880, and made its final trip on September 5, 1923. There were eight scheduled stops along the way: from the origination point at the depot in Old Orchard to the campgrounds, Baty's Cottage, Oceana Avenue, Kinney Shores (just after the trestle crossing Goosefare Brook), the Bay View House, Ferry Beach Park, Grovemore, and Camp Ellis. (Elaine Peverly, from *The Dummy; The Pine Tree State's Seaside Railroad* (1973))

An early history of the area states: "One of the attractions of Old Orchard has always been the charming drive along the shore. This however, could only be enjoyed at low tide and by those who could afford the luxury of a private carriage. But to meet the demands of the general public, and bring this enjoyable recreation accessible to all, a company of sagacious and enterprising men obtained a charter from last winter's legislature for a railroad from the Dunstan to the Saco River, or long the whole line of Old Orchard Beach." Here a passenger flags down The Dummy at an unscheduled stop. (Elaine Peverly, from *The Dummy; The Pine Tree State's Seaside Railroad* (1973))

Officially known as the Old Orchard Railroad, some of the beddings and pilings of the 3.24 mile stretch of track are still visible today—to those who know where to look. The Dummy line carried as many as fifty thousand passengers a season back and forth from Old Orchard to Camp Ellis in Saco. Maine's only seaside railway, the Dummy Railroad opened in 1880 and ran for forty-three years until the popularity and accessibility of the automobile made it unprofitable to the Boston and Maine Railroad, which owned the line.

For only a 10¢ fare, one could travel the entire length of the line in about twenty minutes. The Dummy made about twenty-three round trips per day between Old Orchard and Camp Ellis, making stops along the way at Atlantic Avenue, Union Street, the Campground Station, Ocean Park, Kinney Shores, Grovemore, and Camp Ellis. One could ride the tiny train between the hours of 6:30 a.m. and 10:30 p.m. and many people who worked along the waterfront in Camp Ellis would take it to and from work. By the turn of the century, the Dummy was earning the Boston and Maine Railroad nearly $2,500 per season. (Elaine Peverly, from *The Dummy; The Pine Tree State's Seaside Railroad* (1973))

The tracks that supported the engine were 4 feet 8 1/2 inches wide, and the original was similar to the Metropolitan streetcar engines, which made less noise and burned less coke. The name "Dummy" is believed to have been used to describe the quietness with which the train traveled, refering to the name commonly used for deaf people of the era. (Elaine Peverly, from *The Dummy; The Pine Tree State's Seaside Railroad* (1973))

Riding the Dummy was a very informal affair. Its open-air cars had cane-backed seats, which could be positioned to face either way, on both sides of a center aisle. It made its regular scheduled stops at stations and platforms along the way, but the wave of a hanky or a shrill whistle could stop the train for boarding at any point along the course. (Elaine Peverly, from *The Dummy; The Pine Tree State's Seaside Railroad* (1973))

At a maximum speed of 10 miles per hour, the Dummy was not necessarily a ride for thrill seekers. It was probably one of the safest trains in all of America, but in 1917, the silent locomotive took its only life: a grocery delivery boy, who was driving a Model T on to the tracks at the Atlantic Avenue crossing, was blindsided by the Dummy. He was killed instantly, and his car was dragged for more than a block before the engineer could stop the train. (Steve Fregeau)

Eventually the train's components were updated with a regular small gauge steam engine and larger cars (the cars were still about one third the size of regular cars). Frequently a nervous traveler, fearful of being carried past a destination, would pull on the "fare-register" cord, ringing up another passenger, in an attempt to signal the driver to stop. Often, passengers returning to Old Orchard from Camp Ellis would hang their catch of the day from the platform railings. (Steve Fregeau and Elaine Peverly, from *The Dummy; The Pine Tree State's Seaside Railroad* (1973))

From the termination point in Camp Ellis, passengers were able to take excursion boats to points up the Saco River or across the river to Biddeford Pool or Wood Island. Because there was no turnaround or roundhouse at either end, the Dummy would have to back up the entire length of track from Camp Ellis to the station at Old Orchard. On the return trip a conductor would stand at the back (front) of the last car, directing the engineer with signals from a "pea whistle." (Steve Fregeau)

BEGINING OF 10 MILE RACE
OLD ORCHARD, ME.

Gentlemen, start your engines. Shortly after the Great Old Orchard Fire of 1907, it was thought that automobile racing on the beach would be the boost the town needed. Local drivers, drivers "from away", and people who had never driven before raced on the beach at low tide for years in the early 1900s. Professional drivers, some as famous as Barney Oldfield (in 1903 he became the first man to travel a mile a minute), raced at the beach. Grandstands were built to accommodate the spectators. Sometimes crowds of several thousand people would gather to cheer on their favorites. (Old Orchard Beach Historical Society)

Drivers would start from near the pier and race in a long loop that took them around Googin's Rocks in Ocean Park and then back through the pilings of the pier to a point up the beach. (Steve Fregeau)

It is hard to imagine automobile racing on the beach today, but in the early part of the twentieth century it was commonplace. (Steve Fregeau)

Louis Disbrow's 2-mile-a-minute car. It is doubtful that even this automobile could travel 120 mph—especially on the soft sand of Old Orchard. (Steve Fregeau)

A long way from Indianapolis. (Steve Fregeau)

(Old Orchard Beach Historical Society)

Seven

Horsin' Around

The Kite Track, so named for its figure-eight configuration (making it look somewhat like a kite), was the brainchild of Milland F. Porter, a hotel man and merchant. In this late 1940s photograph one can see the odd shape of the track; the horses have just passed the "intersection" at the small end. Built for speed, the soft marshy surface was topped by nearly a foot of clay to make it easier on the horses' feet. The last meet held here was on July 3, 1950. (Steve Fregeau)

The 1940s were a romantic time in harness racing. Old Orchard Beach was part of the "Grand Circuit," a harness racing tour that included stops in Lexington, Kentucky, Springfield, Illinois, Goshen, New York, and DuQuoin, Canada. For three weeks every summer from late July through the middle of August, the Kite Track was one of the greatest racing stops in North America. (Old Orchard Beach Historical Society)

Located off Walnut Street, behind Guay's Cottages, the Kite Track was one of the most popular draws to Old Orchard in the 1930s and '40s. According to the *Portland Press Herald*, "More money was spent at the track in three weeks than was spent at the all the other attractions in all of Old Orchard for an entire season." (Old Orchard Beach Historical Society)

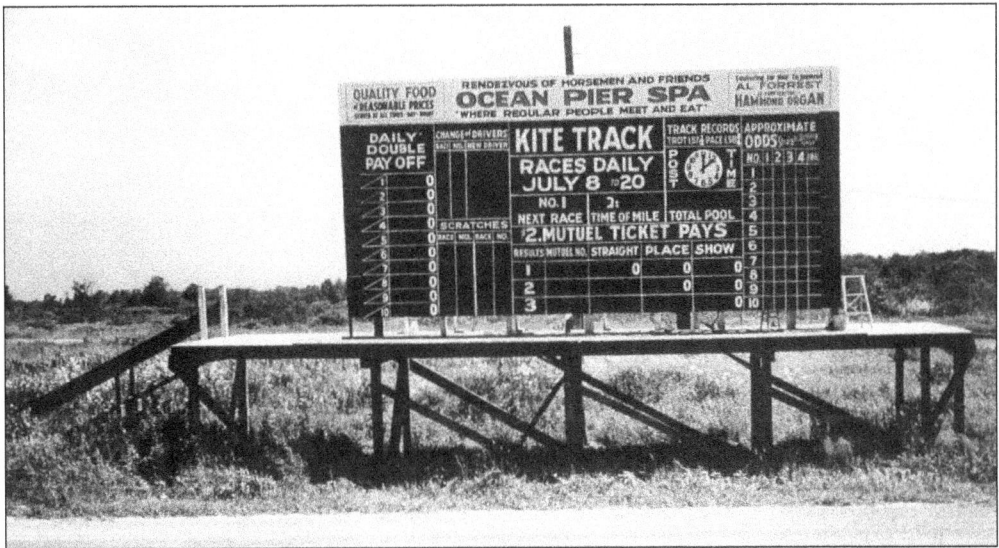

The tote board tells the story. Some of the best drivers in the country were racing at the Kite Track. Horses arrived at the train depot and were then paraded to the track. The fastest horses in harness racing made Old Orchard one of the best stops on the circuit. (Old Orchard Beach Historical Society)

When the Kite Track had outlived its usefulness, the grandstands were razed and the lights were moved to the just-opened Scarborough Downs. But in the 1940s, the Kite Track was so highly regarded for its speed that the most prestigious harness race in all of America, the Hambletonian, considered Old Orchard for its home. (Old Orchard Beach Historical Society)

Maine Sunday Telegram reporter Meryle Cutler wrote: "Women attended these races. Dressed in long waisted, long gowns and carrying dainty lace-edged parasols, they added color to the gay time." Racing at the Kite Track began in the late 1880s and lasted until the early 1900s, until the antiquated betting laws in Maine forced the track's decline. Low attendance by the local race fans also contributed to the demise of racing in Old Orchard. In 1930 Maine adopted the popular pari-mutuel betting system and that revived racing again in Old Orchard. In the 1940s the Kite Track got a face-lift: the number of stables were increased, parking was expanded, and the sport grew through the 1940s until the end of the decade, when the track began to show its age. The clay surface of the track began to get too soft and started breaking up, and it became a hazard for the horses and drivers alike. According to Gerald Coffin, who ran the photo finish at the track, and later moved on to Scarborough Downs, "Not too many people were concerned when the Old Orchard track closed. Scarborough Downs had just opened up and they were running the more popular thoroughbreds." (Old Orchard Beach Historical Society)

Eight

In the Mood

The name of Old Orchard was known far and wide by all of the biggest names in music. From Rudy Vallee's many performances dating from the mid-1920s to the rock and roll bands of the 1950s, the Casino at the end of the pier was one of the "must play" arenas for musicians of all types. It didn't really matter who was playing at the pier: whether it was the house band or a nationally known act, the pier was the place to be on a hot summer night. (Old Orchard Beach Historical Society)

When the band was cookin' the Casino would sway like palm tree in the tropical winds. Between nationally known acts, various house bands would play three concerts a day. (Old Orchard Beach Historical Society)

In addition to dancing and music, the Casino was host to such entertainment as beauty contests. Here the Lee Russell Orchestra plays for the Miss Old Orchard Beach pageant. Notice the three judges (in white suits) eyeing the contestants. (Old Orchard Beach Historical Society)

Jimmy Dorsey. (Old Orchard Beach Historical Society)

Guy Lombardo. (Old Orchard Beach Historical Society)

Benny Goodman.
(Old Orchard Beach
Historical Society)

Duke Ellington. (Old Orchard
Beach Historical Society)

Vaughn Monroe. (Old Orchard Beach Historical Society)

Rudy Vallee on the beach. Just a regular guy by day, he was America's favorite crooner by night, and he packed 'em in for more than a decade. A native of Westbrook, Maine, Vallee loved to come home every year. In the late 1920s there was no singer in America more popular than Vallee. (Teofila Macdonald)

Louis Armstrong and his band. Armstrong appeared in Old Orchard every year for more than a decade. Dave Glovsky (better known as "Dave the Guesser"), a staple at Old Orchard Beach's midway since the 1940s, recalled his friendship with Louis Armstrong in an interview with the *Boston Globe* in 1991: "Louis was playing here back in 1954 and he wanted me to guess his weight, which was 176. He came over in 1955 and he'd gained 9 or 10 pounds, and the next year he'd gained another 10 pounds and I said, 'Lou, how come you're gaining weight?' and he said in that low, gravelly voice, 'Must be all that good ol' Italian spaghetti.' " Even though Armstrong and his band were popular worldwide, he and other black musicians had a hard time finding lodging during their stay in Old Orchard. The 1940s and '50s were a time of segregation in America and Maine was no exception. (Old Orchard Beach Historical Society)

OLD ORCHARD PIER

Movies EVERY Aft. and Eve.
Dancing EVERY Eve. except Sun.

ONE ADMISSION TO BOTH

SATURDAY, JULY 16
ARRANGER AND ORGANIZER OF RAY NOBLE AND DORSEY BANDS
GLEN MILLER AND HIS ORCHESTRA
40c Admission

4 Days starting MONDAY, JULY 18
FROM STATION K Y W THAT MADE JAN SAVITT AND
THE "TOP HATTERS" FAMOUS
FRANK LITTLEFIELD
AND HIS MUSIC
25c 7 to 7:30---40c after
EXTRA! Wed. Old-fashioned Waltz Contest

FRIDAY, JULY 22
RUDY VALLEE
(In Person) And Company
85c 7 to 7:30---$1.10 after (tax included)

Free Dancing Lessons every morning, 10 - 11

Streamline Train to Portland every Nite after
Dance. 35c Round Trip, Portland to O.O. Beach.

(Old Orchard Beach Historical Society)

The house band, the Harder Downing Orchestra. (Old Orchard Beach Historical Society)

Another house band, the Lee Russell Orchestra. Trumpet player John Trull (at right) was the leader of the band. Trull was the first band director at Old Orchard Beach High School and the band room at the high school is named after him. He was the father of Jack Trull, teacher and former football coach at Old Orchard Beach High School, who won three state championships for the Seagulls. (Alice and Jack Trull)

Band director John Trull leads the Old Orchard Beach High School Marching Band in a concert at the square during Memorial Day celebrations in 1953. This location is still popular for concerts of all kinds. (Alice and Jack Trull)

116

Nine

For Your Amusement

Peck's Prancing Ponies. This was a "merry-go-straight." Patrons hopped upon their favorite wooden horse for a trip around the ride. Sort of a combination rollercoaster and merry-go-round, riders could race around the track. Notice the women riding side-saddle. (Steve Fregeau)

Ice cream, soda, and Moxie were all available at this concession stand at Seaside Park. Located where the current Palace Playland is today, Seaside Park was one of the grandest amusement parks on the east coast, and at the turn of the century it was known as the Coney Island of the Northeast. (Old Orchard Beach Historical Society)

The entrance to Old Orchard's Scenic Railway. (Old Orchard Beach Historical Society)

The rowing pond at Seaside Park. On the right is the race track for Peck's Prancing Ponies. (Old Orchard Beach Historical Society)

The Jack Rabbit Rollercoaster. One of the largest rollercoasters on the east coast, the Jack Rabbit was a landmark in Old Orchard for years. This photograph shows the arcade in front of the rollercoaster. The mammoth wooden structure narrowly escaped a fire that wiped out several buildings in the center of this picture. (Jim Pate)

Kiddieland. Much like Palace Playland today, Kiddieland was full of amusements for the younger set. Note the majestic Old Orchard House in the background. The boardwalk extends for hundreds of yards. (Steve Fregeau)

Noah's Ark and the Jack and Jill Slide. (Steve Fregeau)

The Jack Rabbit Rollercoaster. This daring ride was built in 1925. The first rollercoaster in Old Orchard was built in 1914 but burned after the 1923 season. (Steve Fregeau)

Winter wonderland. (Steve Fregeau)

The entrance to Seaside Park. (Steve Fregeau)

Haviland's Bazaar. The entrance to the maze at Haviland's Bazaar was a busy place in the summer time. The Old Orchard Town Hall is in the background of this photograph; note the trolley car to the right of the town hall. (Old Orchard Beach Historical Society)

What amusement park would be complete without a first-class merry-go-round? The first licensed merry-go-round in the town of Old Orchard opened in 1892.

124

Ten

All Around the Town

Daily life in Old Orchard Beach at the turn of the twentieth century. This scene is looking down East Grand Avenue. (Old Orchard Beach Historical Society)

The Old Orchard Town Hall, the post office, and St. Margaret's Catholic Church. (Old Orchard Beach Historical Society)

Looking up Old Orchard Street. Note the fire hydrant in the lower right: the strange couplings on the hydrants were one of the main causes for the amount of devastation of the town during the Great Old Orchard Fire of 1907. (Old Orchard Beach Historical Society)

World Heavyweight Champion Gene Tunney (at center) was a frequent guest at the Old Orchard House. (Old Orchard Beach Historical Society)

While Old Orchard was a place to play for some, others had to work and work hard. Saco's Ray Boutet is caught by a photographer on Old Orchard Street. Photographers would snap pictures of tourists and then try to sell them the photographs. (Nanci Boutet and Ruth Goodale Boutet)

www.ingramcontent.com/pod-product-compliance
Lightning Source LLC
Chambersburg PA
CBHW050710110426
42813CB00007B/2147

* 9 7 8 1 5 3 1 6 0 8 5 1 4 *